COLD

THIEF

PLACE

COLD THIEF PLACE

ESTHER LIN

Alice James Books

New Gloucester, Maine • alicejamesbooks.org

10 9 8 7 6 5 4 3 2 1

Alice James Books are published by Alice James Poetry Cooperative, Inc.

Alice James Books
Auburn Hall
60 Pineland Drive, Suite 206
New Gloucester, ME 04260
www.alicejamesbooks.org

Library of Congress Cataloging-in-Publication Data

Names: Lin, Esther, author.
Title: Cold thief place / Esther Lin.
Other titles: Cold thief place (Compilation)
Description: New Gloucester, Maine : Alice James Books, [2025]
Identifiers: LCCN 2024041989 (print) | LCCN 2024041990 (ebook) | ISBN
  9781949944709 (trade paperback) | ISBN 9781949944426 (epub)
Subjects: LCSH: Noncitizens--United States--Poetry. | Immigrant
  families--United States--Poetry. | Autobiographical poetry, American. |
  LCGFT: Confessional poetry. | Poetry.
Classification: LCC PS3612.I4968 C65 2025 (print) | LCC PS3612.I4968
  (ebook) | DDC 811/.6--dc23/eng/20240924
LC record available at https://lccn.loc.gov/2024041989
LC ebook record available at https://lccn.loc.gov/2024041990

Alice James Books gratefully acknowledges support from individual donors, private
foundations, the National Endowment for the Arts, and the Poetry Foundation
(https://www.poetryfoundation.org).

ART WORKS.

Cover art: Detail from "Bildnis einer jungen Frau mit Flügelhaube" (1440) by Rogier
van der Weyden. Staatliche Museen zu Berlin, Gemäldegalerie / Christoph Schmidt.
Public Domain.

TABLE OF CONTENTS

Why you want to go to this cold thief place?

—Jean Rhys

COLD THIEF PLACE

The prophet knew
I could be deported.

But he said my soul as well
as my body could suffer.

What did I fear more?
A fire clawing

its way along my rug.
Offering me what I love best.

Or a man at the door asking
quietly my name, my date of birth.

THE GHOST WIFE

Who, after years
with her husband,
years of rearing
their strapping boy,
is scorched by an eye.
She was gathering laundry.
The sun stuttered
from the clouds.
The rice bubbled
on the stove. Her hands
and face bubbled
too. She did not
cry out. She did not
speak. She was hurried
indoors. What to do?
The neighbors. The talk.
The thing to do was
lay her in a coffin
upstairs
and close the lid.

Such wives were
revered by my grandmother
and her grandmother.
Who knows what single
women thought? Single—
the sickly, the ugly,
or kept back
to tend aging parents.
A role my mother prepared
me for. To fold sheets.
Call credit card companies.
Make light chatter. Drive.
She died suddenly,
before she could enjoy
this. Three years later
I did the unthinkable:
I married. According
to the folk tales,
it is not the union
of inhuman to human
that is the great metaphor.
You are not nothing
before you marry.
Rather, you are simply
one without a story.
Become a wife.
That is a metamorphosis
worthy of legend.

鬼   guǐ

My father is
patient. He
inscribes a character
on my palm as he
names the glyphs.
A face, a tail,
another tail.
He did this
when I was small
and reluctant.
Today I can read
six characters.
My name. *Home.*
Nation. Love. Door.
But I liked the tickle
of language on my palm,
that my father did this
because his grandfather did,
to save paper and ink
in the land he calls
the prairies
of South China.
A face, a tail, a tail.
It means *a ghost, a fiend,*
a derogatory term,
my father's preferred
phrase for Americans.

Guǐ is always
foreign. *To return.*
To deceive. To overawe.
To be the one
who overawes.
I write this
without certainty,
to the one
who overawes me.

It's my sister who
authorizes that mother
be unplugged.
My father and I
don't go with her.
She leaves, then returns
silent. The next day
she wants to watch
the latest zombie program.
A man can't bring himself
to shoot his wife
as she wanders the streets.
Dead, she remains
lovely. Dress damp,
feet bare as if
returned from a party,
pumps slipped off
and left in the foyer.
The man readies himself
at the second-story window
with a chair and rifle.
She stands on the blacktop.
She is looking at the door.
Hello my love.
Will you open up?
At the credits my father
leans back, clears
his throat. He says,
I can tell one better.

HIDDEN ONE

An angel told my mother of my coming.
I heard this story again and again: the mortal

in light gingham, hair beneath a veil
like the blue-eyed Israelite wives on TV.

Hands clasped over her holy belly.
God has heard. You will be the mother of Samuel.

This was Brazil. Christ the Redeemer
blazed opposite green mountains,

less green each year by dotting favelas.
My mother lived in the rich valley. The sweat

that clung to her collarbone her own making.
Mother of a prophet. She liked that.

When the doctors said *girl,* she changed my name
from Samuel to Esther. Prophet to concubine.

Savior of a people my mother didn't care for.
Esther was not summoned. Her great deed

was going forward, regardless.
My mother didn't hold me for two days.

Once, she believed she was the flame-headed
child of commonplace parents, about to slip

into her glory as she would an evening gown.
Socialite. Painter. Missionary.

Matrimony was her genius.
She married to defect from China.

To a man already married, his wife
so meek my mother mistook her

for the family servant.
Esther. The name means *hidden one*.

Samuel was eleven when he heard the call.
He woke in his little chamber in the rear

of the temple and answered,
Speak, Lord, for your servant hears.

My mother knew no call would come for me.
No flame would burnish my brow.

If I am a prophet, I am one who divines
what has already passed. My sight is unclear,

the entrails rarely auspicious.

I SEE HER BEST

when she's half-hidden.
As if my eyelids were mother's skirts.
When there's darkness like a kerosene lamp's.
Hair glossy as a catfish flank.
A lone woman released from China
to join her fiancé in Vietnam.
When abandoned, seducing a married man.
When cast out, crossing borders,
a silent river raft in purple twilight.
To meet my father, for the first time.
He—more beautiful than she.
When split by cancer, asking my father
and her new lover to pray together.
Red Guard. Red tape.
What facts. What luck.
A xeroxed photo in my desk.
1974. A young woman clasping the arm
of a married man, her wrapped hair
and secret smile, her face, or a version of the face
I touch in my sleep. I don't claim anything.
Not because I don't believe in ways of survival,
but my imagination is small.
Metastasis and blood count.
They don't say *disembowel*, but that's what they did.
Colostomy. Hysterectomy.
A legal miracle, my history professor said
of the flight from China. *Millions starving,
and your mother gets married.*

THE REAL THING

for Janine Joseph

In a car traveling from New York to Virginia,
a dealer, a dealer, a stranger, my brother, and myself.
I sat between the stranger and my brother
because everyone smoked out the windows
and because I was a girl. We drove the I-95.
*Your English is so good. How can you
be illegal?* the dealers laughed.
I was seventeen. My brother refused to speak.
The dealers drove us to a lawyer's dining room.
The lawyer notarized our proof of address.
4 Lachine Lane, Alexandria.
In French La Chine means China. In China
4 is an inauspicious number.
In Alexandria the poems of Sappho burned.
The dealers drove to the DMV. *Don't speak
English. We're your translators,* the dealers warned me.
If you speak English, you will fuck this up.
I passed the written exam. My brother passed
the written exam. The stranger failed.
He would have to make this journey again
in six months time. He wanted a refund.
I wanted to sit by a window for the ride back.
My brother refused to speak.
The learner's permit was a dot matrix printout.
The lawyer would forward the dealers the real thing.
The dealers would forward my father the real thing.
It's not even the real thing, the stranger shouted.

OUT OF THE MOUTHS OF BABES

In 1992 my mother believed
the world was going to end.
Having given this church
cash and also her wedding ring—
sign of new fidelity—
she asked in the parking lot,
Is it better to be
citizens of Heaven
or of the United States?
Ten years old, I knew well
enough what to say.
Then she called the caseworker.
And this is how my siblings and I
remained illegal.

UP THE MOUNTAINS DOWN THE FIELDS

slogan of the Chinese Cultural Revolution, 1966–76

Strange
to think of you
Mother
cheeks bright
with the nuisance
of revolution
thin hands
rosy fingertips
levering yourself
onto the train
that would bring you
to Wuping
or did you go
by foot
dressed in flannels
and broadcloth
as one of your
future husbands
tells me
I can only see you
in your favorite
dove-brown
wool suit
Jackie O. style
to the office
when pain
kept you

home we ate
bonchon chicken
our last meal
before Booth
Memorial
oh yes cancer
oh yes genetic
percentage
but you were warmly
dressed in Wuping

one hundred
fifty rural miles
west of your
native Xiamen
a midsize city
I googled today
fresh-faced
cybercafes
bookshops
you and your
university pals
sent as operators
of Mao's
Great Leap Forward
to till soil
teach letters
but when I say
strange I mean
how you were like
the revolution
itself
always spoiling
for the next account
next man
next fight
when I say
strange I mean
how even as
you were dying

and I asked
what were
the happiest
of your days
and you didn't say
us I knew that
already
I didn't mind
but you said
the revolution
nobody
says that

after you died
I remembered
Odysseus
and his bowl of blood
so he could speak
to his mother
three embraces
into air but then
her voice uttering
does it matter
in Wuping
what you loved
was the tunes
and *unity*
little care
why or how
you played violin
your friend guitar
and evenings
you all sang
until the sun
dwindled
candles kerosene
were too dear
to burn for
fervor alone
surely you were
cold those nights
on your cot

in the newly
built hut
and if you had
companionship
my father
doesn't know
I forget that
you were at most
twenty-two
I thought I would
rather go down
and face those
three dogs
than hear you
say more

rosy fingers
is a phrase
I learned reading
D'Aulaires' Book
of Greek Myths
my brother stole
Prometheus-
style from the
school library
the goddess
Eos would
wake the world
with rosy fingers
at six I didn't know
metaphor
that *rosy fingers*
meant *morning rays*
I imagined
her fingers as yours
touching gliding
my hair
in the recumbent
hills most remote
meadow of me
when I think
of happiness
I still think
of D'Aulaires'
lithographs

river gods rising
fleet-footed nymphs
the night-cool
inside my body
a secret

did we share
this too
our bodies
houses for our
best stories
did you sing songs
of redistribution
while dreaming
of Anna Karenina's
black ball gown
while you worked
the fields
of rice and yams
fields flooded
under a low-
burning sky
when I learned
though not
through you
you hid handwritten
copies of
favorite chapters
Tolstoy
Wharton
Flaubert
all forbidden
under your pillow
on that cot
I felt so pleased

and then guilt
for being so pleased
good capitalist
maybe it was
a downward-
plunging woman
with her crown
of dark curls
that gave you hope
but for what
your future
would be us
and a near
lifetime of new
powerlessness
well
you seemed happy
before you died
too happy
you were joining
those young corpses
with their
laudanum
drownings
leaps into cruel
exquisite air
what hurts me
is that I'd read
these books only
after

should I say
you beat us
too
in the shower
in public
on the face
with boots
with a chair leg
chased Vicky
to cut her
awful hair
told us
get work done
more tits
less chin
more eyes
less ears
but it's verging
on melodrama
nice people
don't suspend
their disbelief

maybe you
were quelling
the latest uprising
that was us
babies
kicking children
unspeaking adults
without
the Little Red Book
the task of
whom to love
and how
could you know
what to do
I was last-born
like so many
last-born daughters
in China Korea Vietnam
in Flushing
we're raised
to be workhorses
well Mother
I'm working now

I have
deformed you
primed much
and painted little
perhaps in the after
you can meet anyone
you can meet
the *you* I've made
in this poem
you can judge
each other
from afar
then self-love
brings you close
laughter or snort
I don't know
twin of my mother
don't speak to me
anymore

maybe
your long gone
days were
happiest
because while
you had
the cold fields
and a song
you had
the cold fields
and a song

WHEN ICE CAME FOR ME

In the caves of Lascaux,
this is what I thought.

Not huge bison,
balancing on dainty legs,

not cats rising from low-slung bellies.
Not even the single hand

blazing out of twenty thousand years.
I was a woman out of time

and place. Illegal immigrants
do not go to France. In our history,

there is no preliterate woman
crouched right here, fingers

dipped in red and ochre pigment
she'd ground by day,

and someone at her side,
holding the light. Always,

someone kindling her brow
with that light.

In a dream
the registrar lobby is packed.

A uniform tells us, *No one leave.*
ICE is doing their work.

My professor—you know
the one—says nothing.

Identification is demanded.
Lines form.

Rendering an animal
on eight legs instead of four,

the guide says, gives a static image
the appearance of movement.

A flickering torch causes
the animals to race across the walls.

Horned aurochs follow me.
Two, four, six, each checking

the other. Rhinoceros.
Last come the lions, female and male,

on eight legs.
This is how I flee.

My legs doubled, then tripled,
in the place where I should not be.

I piss and I bleed here.
All around me, animals leap.

DISAPPEARING ACT

The young man yanked up
the chain-link so I could crawl,
skirt and all, into Cypress Hills
Cemetery, where the borough's
only fox strolled out a limestone
mausoleum and the homeless
rest here too. We visited
the Houdini family, stepping
over pyramids of stones,
offerings of playing cards, flowers.
He was young. I was illegal.
Which meant to keep on living
in America I had to marry
a nice boy—all explained
as we shivered with the magician,
laid in the earth called Machpelah,
place of two portions.
The sky wide as paper,
us and the centuries dead
before the first snowfall of the year,
first arrest by Enforcement
and Removal. He understood
as well as any natural-born American:
something about three children
showing up at Kennedy—
wrong stamps, wrong paperwork,
a father losing three homes
in the old country, a mother
keen to say she'd made it

in America. He listened,
he listened more, he asked:
To make all that happen
what are you willing to do.
I straightened. I straightened the flowers,
the cards, the stones. I said:
To make all that happen
what are *you* willing to do.
Over the horizon, two hills down,
a stranger walks ahead of me.
Head bowed, hands in her coat,
she crosses the Interboro,
weaving the same way I will,
car after car after car.
Red taillights playing across her back
just as they will on mine.

MS. L— DESCRIBE YOUR PETITIONER

Like me, my petitioner has never left
the United States. He says he has no need,
he is happy and has no needs.
My petitioner is interested in sex.
His distinguishing feature is a hibiscus tattoo.
My petitioner's mother dislikes me.
Her son would never marry someone like me.
He doesn't argue with her, he is not an arguer, he says.
My petitioner is not often home.
My petitioner and I met in a utopian studies class.
My petitioner and I met in Anglo-Saxon poetry.
My petitioner and I stopped having sex after six months.
My petitioner and I have sex twice a week.
The agent at Homeland Security asks why
I wanted my petitioner to be my petitioner.
The truth is my father saved three thousand dollars,
the market rate for men
who petition for illegal women.

MR. F— DESCRIBE YOUR BENEFICIARY

So studious, so good,
my beneficiary accomplishes all she sets out to.
Forms, bills, lawyers.
My beneficiary loves to play.
Her big toe pinning my cock
just so, just as I've described, *Now make that face,*
I say, and she does. On my back,
blood in my mouth, her hands around
my neck, how hard she concentrates!
So give her
what she wants, ma'am,
and then she'll wipe me down.

DONE RIGHT

One bed, squared-off sheets.
One toothbrush, pearl-blue,
one toothbrush, pink.
The petitioner shuts the door
and hangs his hat.
The beneficiary says,
It's time to lie down.
The petitioner says,
All right. Yes.
It has to be done right.
One rococo print.
One belt. One collared shirt.
Draped over
the wicker chair.
Come lie down.
Are you going to do it right?
Oak table, garage sale.
One woman's dress, not
ironed. One sock.
Where is the other?
Pages of names,
occupations, allegiance.
Everything in its
place. Mist from the beneficiary's
shower. Does she love
the petitioner?
She steps out, damp as a frog.
The petitioner's throat
is parched. Will she

pour a glass? One
tumbler, crystal.
Ring of hard water.
White soap.
A note has been made.
A note has been made.

THE BADLANDS

Say drive across the desert and see
jewel sky and white limestone,

the land so long you can roll and roll
always toward the same hill. This is escape

or so Hollywood claims. In a western,
a man races a dying child through

starlight and saguaro and fires his gun
to rouse a doctor, and who is more

relieved when she is saved? A woman
stands in a crowded hall, says her daughter

has evaded coyotes, has wandered for days.
She lived. The woman does not describe rock

or brush. She does not even mention the thirst,
the vomiting. She sits, exhausted by her story.

Her story is not my story. It is the one
you hear first. From the news, from someone

you know. It *is* someone you know.
Once I drove to California with my first

husband, a gray-eyed student I married
not for love. Everyone has advice

about the Jucumba Wilderness, where
the light is sore and the road burns black.

Turn off the air-conditioner. Lower
the windows as the car climbs.

Overheat, and there's no help for miles.
But the wilderness held a tollbooth, a pistol,

and Raphael, who leaned into the car
and asked, Are you an American citizen?

Do you have photo ID? Raphael, who might
be handsome in another uniform. While my

good husband passed over the hard, iridescent
card, the one that declared permanent resident

alien, Raphael peered into my twilight face.
You sure you're Brazilian?

To be asked a question and have an answer.
This was my first taste of paradise.

FOR MY FATHER THE WEST BEGINS
IN AFRICA

But what is a Chinaman to do with Africa,
I hear you ask, on the great green waters that separate

the forests of Madagascar from Mozambique Island,
where half a million women and men walked down

stone ramps into waiting ships?
In 1965, my father paid four hundred and thirty dollars

to board a cargo ship in Hong Kong and follow the old
trade route that ends in the sugar fields of Brazil.

The *Ruys* made the familiar stops—Cape Town,
Durban, and here, Mozambique: Chinese passengers

stepping out of steerage, Chinese passengers
marveling the island's fort of whitewashed stone,

cannon guns, and outside its pitched rampart,
gentle waters. But my father doesn't tell me this.

Neither does Lonely Planet, which calls it
the finest military building on the continent,

without mention of the clever men who designed
tunnels and pens to keep the enslaved unseen

by the public. Of the public, my father reports the whites
were *not very welcoming,* but *there were many trees.*

It was clean, ordinary. He saw Black people
for his first time. *At least they weren't slaves anymore,*

he says with a sort of shrug, the tranquility of a man
who, at age eight, watched a Japanese soldier slice

the head off a boy with a single stroke.
This, he says, *was how they knew their swords*

were sharp. So I don't know what bondage
means to him. How can I ask?

In 1794, the *São José* sailed out of the same port
as my father, made the same stop in Mozambique.

Then near Cape Town, in those famed currents,
high winds, the ship *came apart.* Of the enslaved,

pressed flesh to flesh with their backs on the floor,
over two hundred perished.

For my father, the West begins in Africa. He entered
a new history; one in which his own would be made blank.

I finally met men who were as tall as me.
Who I could look in the eye. I felt comfortable.

He was thirty years old, younger than I am now
as he shows me, palms down, elbows at right angles,

how violent the waves at the approach to Cape Town,
how his ship rose and plunged—

It felt like a cold wind inside your stomach.
A lot of people were sick. Not me.

His wonder still fresh, like a child's, for his own time.
Which fifty years ago was still to come—

when that young man would not be ruled
by the Empire of Japan or the Red Guard,

famines or beatings or heartbreak, but could hope
for a wife, three children, a Volkswagen and a corner office,

even the simple pleasure of not being always the tallest,
and he left Cape Town with some regret.

The *Times* reports that after the remaining survivors
of the *São José* were dragged or pushed ashore,

within two days, they were sold again.

IN DURBAN WE ENCOUNTERED
A PROBLEM

So when we went to the post office,
we didn't know what to do.

European or Black. Which window?
We discussed, we joined

the Black queue. Then a clerk
ran—really ran!—waving us

to the European window.
My father and three more Chinese,

frayed and unwashed, not so much
men but chaff carried on wind

to this land of trees and light and two
of everything. I'd like to think

my father shook his head. Said,
Sir, I'm fine right here.

Did he know that he would keep going?
Farther than South Africa. Farther than

Brazil. To snowfall. New York.
Where he must shovel and salt the walk,

haul a dryer into the alley, stoop
and repair it. That his heart

would fail. Two weeks in a city hospital
changed him. The morning he drove back

to the laundromat, the sky white with ice,
he thought of his brothers, sisters, his mother

left behind. What he could have done.
Why he didn't. Which queue did he choose

that day in Durban? Surely he imagined
the invitation boded well.

FIRST SNOW

My mother bought us matching
maroon coats for the event. New

to such clothes, I zipped right into
the wool of my scarf. Last child out.

The hedge held me like a box.
It would burst brilliant pink one day—

my first flowers in the northern hemisphere.
Today it stood puffy with something

limp and indolent, the way it lay
across the stems. With a bare finger

I poked and poked while beyond
my sister and brother shrieked,

trying to build the snowman they knew
was expected of them. It was mostly mud.

Even though snow fell everywhere.
The pavement, the cars. My mother's

hair. The beautiful country.
That's what the Chinese call America.

We must have appeared odd.
Three children in identical coats, looking
around in disbelief.

AZALEAS

appear in all the early photos.
My arms belted around my mother,
only the top of my head seen
because she has spoken sharply
and now resorts to begging.
Your father hasn't seen you
in eight weeks. Smile. Smile!
I am too sad or sick to obey
and she makes that sound
between her teeth that
signals the end of a unit
of patience. I release her
and dash off. What follows
is probably hell, I don't
remember anymore. Only after,
dawdling along the hedge,
touching the little flaring flowers.
There are so many that as I run
my hand along, I meet more,
nothing else. The top of my head
is hot from sun. I understand
I am two girls. The one my mother
wants and the one who lives only
among her own kind.

A BOOK ABOUT DRAGONS

for Laurence Yep

Because we loved God, I could not
tell my mother that the most wonderful

phrase I'd read was not from the Bible
but a book about dragons.

A heroine and an exile, my dragon
called her home the *Green Darkness*.

Like the dragon I longed for the Green Darkness.
Not for the green or the dark, but the conundrum

of its name: a spirit so rich it must occupy
two bodies. The word as body. Wasn't this

another way of saying *mother, child*.
I experienced it in the deep, attending

nature of books. The book and me.
I felt it later too. With Jane as she walked

past Thornfield. And in Combray. By then
my mother was dead and still

I could not tell her about the wonderful
things I'd read.

FANTASY NOVEL

The first book I bought
with my own money. So I cried
when she tore the garnet
cover off.

I had never seen anyone do that.

She tore ten pages out
and tore those in half.
She tore fast, her hands
like well-trained dogs.

My mother was saving my soul.
She alone could protect me.

The book held four hundred and two
pages. Its back cover
Celtic knotwork you could feel
when you ran your hand over it.

The trash can smelled like fresh paper.
Later that afternoon I peeled carrots
for dinner over it.

READING *MADAME BOVARY*

That afternoon Bovary went
to the apothecary's closet,

fumbling for arsenic
to draw out her black bile,

make her mouth a hole.
She waited hours for the worst of it,

the shearing of her dark lovely hair—
though for many years

my mother's hair was not lovely
but thin as sagebrush

an autumn fire had passed over.
There are mothers who demand

a price. Youth. Sex organs
without cancer. She said,

You can't know how bad it is.
Bovary's daughter worked in a satin mill.

There is no talk of her beauty.
To say my mother was not beautiful

when she died is merciless.
Today I am without mercy.

ATTACHMENT THEORY

Once she began spitting,
foam dashing the windshield
like snow, I reached sideways

from the driver's seat and volleyed
my fist against her breastbone.
Twice. More than twice.

Don't hit me!

She cried out in the voice
that belonged to me those Sunday
evenings when she opened

the shower door and beat
my face and chest with an open palm
as soap and water ran.

Now it was a game.
We took turns, the mother demonstrating,
the cub imitating. How to

hurt a person in the way
they allow. Every person allows
for it, sooner or later. My mother

was my first.

DIAGNOSIS

After she died, people admitted
something might have gone awry.
Nerves, suggested one doctor;
narcissism, another. Over lunch
a cousin proposed, *Your mother
had a difficult personality.*
All true and didn't matter. She
nourished us by nourishing us—
she wrapped dumplings of crystal
shrimp, sliced heavy eggplants,
and fish, always one fish
gleaming among the meats and greens.
I hardly ate. It was too rich, too much
of everything. Which annoyed her.
*Why won't you accept what I offer?
I work so hard. Why? Why?*
When my husband tells me
he loves me, I hear her instead.

HABIT

My husband's favorite is to suffer.
I too have taken this up;

I pant for what I can't have.
The world is full of trite regard.

Those who love lightly as houseflies
do so because they expect calamity,

and those who love passionately
demand a righting of ancient wrongs.

My mother did both.
Her voice high and keen

from the bed she routinely took to ill.
I brought her pills; she shared them

with me and I went off into my own life,
fearing and trusting everyone.

CHOLERA IS WHAT MY GRANDFATHER
DID DURING THE WAR

In the summer of 2016, cholera was nowhere
to be found in the great prairie of Saskatchewan,

where my husband and I rode the sleeper from Toronto
all the way west. Something about the train's knock and sway,

its fading grandeur: Art Deco dining car, windows
replaced in the seventies, office carpet in the nineties,

polyester napkins older only than the teenagers who
warmed our meals. Can I say we were happy?

Our first night, we dined with Paul and Charlotte, translators
from the north of England. Also, Morris dancers.

We leaned in to see them on Charlotte's phone—
Morris dancing has uncertain origins, Paul explained.

Perhaps Moorish, like the Italian *moresca*. So lingering
an immigrant in the English countryside

this dance became evidence of one's Englishness.
Chilled wine arrived, then bisque.

We turned to Austen's ten-pound note, the Brontës'
parsonage, lately replicated; they fielded our questions

about that and the Queen and football hooligans.
Then—two Brits, two Americans, what more

would we speak of? "The war," of course, as if it were not
seventy years ago but ten, and we were tasting peace and wealth

as we recounted our hunger, our rations. Our lost boys.
Paul and Charlotte were earnest in a way we could not be,

not me, Brazilian-born, of Chinese descent, reader
of spy novels. Not my husband, a Catholic whose family

left Belfast two generations back, now considered
"American" or "white." No, for our friends, it was simple.

Charlotte's grandfather studied the beaches of Normandy
in advance of D-Day—*O the wild charge they made!*

Something of those Norman beaches breached
must have heartened an old Saxon. Or so I imagined.

Of the great triumphing over the great,
those gleaming boots, black uniforms so smart

Hollywood would dress up for decades
and find America falling in love—

Her grandfather tested sample after sample
of French sands, which beach most capable

of supporting vehicles and mortar and body-falls.
No doubt he was a man who did not hold himself

in high esteem but worked quietly,
celebrated peacetime, was tender to his grandchildren

and forgot his own heroism, though it was not to be forgotten....
We listened with all the pleasure of a bedtime story,

and then I said, My grandfather died of cholera.
He was in China during the war. He died of cholera.

Here in the Art Deco dining car, with pink lamps lit
and the yellow-blooming canola beyond, it sounded

like a punch line. So we laughed.

TELL ME WHERE THE PAST IS

There's one way to talk about beauty
and it hasn't changed since Spanish
ponies, born from wreckage, swam
to become island wildings, alone and
windblown. Feral. American. Hasn't
changed since the vase painter of Attica
chose a flutist and dancer for her subject
in the fire. It's 2014 that I love
this girl on panpipes. She peers down
at her hands at work, one foot hitched up
as if she too were to spring to dance.
But no. The making of this music
pins her to her seat, the black behind her
not the field of the contending mind
but its best warmth, a gift to her
compatriot who works without instrument,
save the spinning dress and upraised arms
elegant in honor of the next time
she would see the flutist and ask her
to play in celebration of their friendship.
And so with my sisters and me, on that
island known for its salt-eating horses,
where we promised to return year after year
for a swim and reminder of what carries us
aloft in the darkening waters, whether it's
refusal or a special imagination on how
to flourish without a mother. *Mother*,
and one glimpses the sacred hair braiding,
laying out of clothes, sacred good mornings.

One sees these things even if there was
none but what a child understands
of capture and release, before and after,
while the sun pinks the beach grass
and the Atlantic grays. And how these
restate all I want to ask about motherlessness,
of how it's possible not to vanish because
she does. I don't mean this as a keening
of grief, though others agree it must be.
The vase painter has long since vanished,
and the two continue practicing their love.
It's that easy, yes?

LISTENING

for Richie Hofmann

Opera troupes came to the village
every summer.

An egg warm in his pocket
my father would run out early

for a good seat. To watch warriors fight.
For the handsprings, backflips.

When maidens sang, he ate,
he waved to his brother.

Upright and bespectacled, his brother
played erhu with the pros.
       An honor.

The lake was made of silk; the moon, too.

Sometimes the swords spun so fast
that in his excitement the egg broke.

His mother strapped him on the legs
and hands, but the next day he did

the same thing.

When all this went away, no one apologized.

A piano gallops.

My brother and father hunch over a tape deck
in the porch room, sun falling on their backs.

> *There. That's the boy. He cries out.*
> *He's singing, "My father, he has hurt me,"*
>
> Tom explains.

Who's hurt him? our father asks.

> *The Elf King.*

In China, the elves meddle too.

Tom's fingers dance triplets on his knee.
Schubert is real. Goethe is real.

Tom, eager to learn something fast and dangerous.

Though no one's called for me, I sit between them,
schoolbag hot on my back.

Dad admires the baritone's vim.
He's heard the French and Italians, he's heard Beethoven and Bach,

but nothing so awful as this.

The baritone plays the father, the boy, and the Elf King.
He has to be really good to sing as all three.

Dad rests his hand on Tom's head, the shiny bowl cut
our mother's made.

We stop, we rewind. To hear it
this time without his schoolboy German,

his faltering Chinese   which our father corrects, gently.

WUPING, 1969

Nights she sat on her bed, hair plaited
and plump beneath a woven scarf, and outside

the emptied fields, the tilted quarry speaking
low the verse she would write to her lover.

1969 was no one's happiness
but hers, when she rode or walked west

to teach reading and writing to farmers,
herders, their children mute and removed

from her as fish beneath the creek's flashing
surface. Hunger, denunciations, these too were

mute and removed as she wrote for her pupils
the basics of the day:

The cock crows, the earth turns white.
How she marched and sang for such rhythms,

how she tended her love during those charred
nights as she considered her line. She listened

and would reach for the page, but not yet.
Not yet to any certainty, when waiting was

a shadow on her cheek and she was moved
at any moment. What were her words of intent,

words of control and that first gentle reaching,
her future held before her

like a cool glass bowl into which she would
wash her face, place aside, stand and dress.

CHU YING

When pregnant

she could not travel to the capital
with her husband.

And so, after he left,
she beat their son.

Dear mother,

I depart to Brazil in May.
See Mr. Wu and ask for his map,
and he will show you where that
is.

At the capital
her husband took a second wife. In 1934,

a man could do this.

Dear mother,

I am in Durban now, for three days.

The bottom of my suitcase
broke. It was a poor idea
to bring all my books,
but I'm afraid I won't be able
to read anything without them. Them
and your letters, of course.

Because her husband left her
before he served the other side

the radicals did not beat her.
But everything else, they did.

Dear mother,

The paulistanos are kind
and unconcerned
with their neighbors.
Some are frugal. Today I sold
two parasols and a baby's
bonnet. A good day.

When the second revolution came

she took pleasure in
denouncing others.

Dear mother,

I am sending you all I can.

News of a grandson pleased her.
A boy brings good tidings,
she replied.

Dear mother,

Remember how every evening
grandfather used to say,

With stars for a shawl, the moon
for a hat, I hurry home.

The Communists and I can't
live under the same sky.

Perhaps my children will visit
but for me, never.

WINTER

In order to see my first
pear tree

I took three trains

to a cloister shipped stone by stone
from Spain to Washington Heights,

then reconstructed to a more perfect whole
enclosing

gardens laid by scholars of tapestry
and stained glass and the poetry of flowers,

and inside one of these
a tree.

❧

Not knowing *cold*
my brother was seized
when he stepped from the plane.

Once an ice pop
shared among three children,

cold could be laid on the kitchen board
and cut carefully by our father—we watched

carefully—into equal pieces
to place into our mouths and suck.

❧

With my husband
I wanted to be as children,
sex a discovery
we could publish, win scientific prizes
for—I stroked his nipple to make it true,
true as children making their way
through a house
until someone bled,
someone got angry and then
we tiptoed.

❧

Before he died
my father said
what no one wished to hear.

We should have stayed.

❧

In place of marble
we weighed stone pine and magnolia,

the difference being *the stone pine
is native to Italy, Lebanon, and Syria*

and *the magnolia evolved*
before the appearance
of bees and my brother stood between

two planters, speckled
in their shade, saying over and over,
I don't know.

They both feel like him, to me.

ILLEGAL IMMIGRATION

is the absence of a paper
and the presence of a person.

A person with pages and pages
documenting her movements

is a convict.
Or undocumented.

Who is made to say, *My name is.*
Who is made to say, *I am the child of.*

Immigration wants to know the names
of your parents. The names of their parents.

A people with lineage can still be scattered.
Is the son of Abraham. Is the son of Isaac. Is the son of Jacob.

People who do not know about documents
do not need them.

They have never needed them.
A person without documents

is the one who must bear them aloft.
They will set her hand on fire.

It takes place in the bathroom
of a border patrol station.

Kingsville, Texas.
All at once, she needs to drink, piss, crap.

Her period comes. The agent says,
No you can't go to your mother.

Illegal immigration began with a law.
It ends with a new law.

She may not step onto a cattle car.
She may die on foot. In the fields.

In labor. In custody.
You know what is happening.

She speaks. She is speaking.
My name is. I am the child of.

See if that works.

NOTES

"The Ghost Wife" refers to a scene in *The Walking Dead*.

"Up the Mountains Down the Fields" draws inspiration from Tracy You's article "China's 'Lost Generation' Recall Hardships of Cultural Revolution," published in CNN.com, Oct. 24, 2012. It speaks of Hu Rongfen, who read *Anna Karenina* and other banned Western novels, during the revolution. I hope the poem honors this particular aspect of Hu's spirit.

The woman in "The Badlands" relates her story in Frederick Wiseman's *In Jackson Heights*.

"For My Father the West Begins in Africa" quotes from Helene Cooper's essay "Grim History Traced in Sunken Slave Ship Found Off South Africa," published in *The New York Times*, May 31, 2015.

"Cholera Is What My Grandfather Did during the War" is dedicated to Paul and Charlotte Clarke, whose remarkable stories I amended to fit the poem.

"Listening" refers to Franz Schubert's Lied "Erlkönig."

"Wuping, 1969" quotes a traditional Chinese verse.

"Tell Me Where the Past Is" refers to a fifth-century BCE calyx-krater called *Berlin Dancing Girl*. Its painter is thought to be Apulian, not Attic. The poem draws its title from John Donne's "Song."

ACKNOWLEDGMENTS

Thank you to the periodicals that published these poems, in varying forms:

Copper Nickel: "I See Her Best"
The Cortland Review: "Tell Me Where the Past Is" and "Habit"
Crab Orchard Review: "Cholera Is What My Grandfather Did during the War," winner of the 2018 Richard Peterson Poetry Prize
Diode: "A Book about Dragons"
Drunken Boat: "Up the Mountains Down the Fields"
Epiphany: "Disappearing Act"
Gulf Coast: A Journal of Literature and Fine Arts: "The Real Thing"
Hyperallergic: "Ms. L—Describe Your Petitioner" and "Mr. F— Describe Your Beneficiary"
Indiana Review: "In Durban We Encountered a Problem"
The Journal: "Cold Thief Place"
Massachusetts Review: "For My Father the West Begins in Africa"
The Missouri Review's Poem of the Week: "The Ghost Wife"
New England Review: "Winter" and "Listening"
Pleiades: Literature in Context: "Illegal Immigration" and "When ICE Came for Me"
Ploughshares: "Reading *Madame Bovary*"
Poem-a-Day, Academy of American Poets: "Azaleas"
Poetry Northwest: "Out of the Mouths of Babes"
Southeast Review: "Diagnosis"
Southern Humanities Review: "Hidden One"
TriQuarterly: "The Badlands"
Vinyl Poetry and Prose: "Wuping, 1969"

"Habit" is featured in *Best New Poets 2022: 50 Poems from Emerging Writers,* edited by Paula Bohince.

Some of the poems in this book appear in *The Ghost Wife*, winner of the 2017 Poetry Society of America's Chapbook Fellowship, selected by Patrick Rosal.

Many thanks to Carey Salerno, Alyssa Neptune, Lacey Dunham, Genevieve Hartman, Julia Bouwsma, and the marvelous staff and board members of Alice James Books.

Thank you to my teachers—Patrick Phillips, for listening closely. John Weir, Kimiko Hahn, Wayne Moreland. Eamon Grennan, who taught me to "lay bare the narrative field." Timothy Donnelly. Nicole Sealey, Jason Koo, Joseph Legaspi, Rachel Eliza Griffiths. And in memory of Eavan Boland.

To editors and judges who supported my work, thank you. Patrick Rosal, Alice Quinn. Keetje Kuipers. Peter LaBerge. Mihaela Moscaliuc and Michael Waters. Alison Williams. And in memory of Jon Tribble.

Thank you to the institutions that gave me that special time to grow: the Wallace Stegner Fellowship program and Stanford University, the Fine Arts Work Center at Provincetown, Cité internationale des arts, Cave Canem, Poets House, and the T. S. Eliot House.

To the friends I've made because of poetry, from the happy long ago and happy now: Antonius-Tín Bui (Sister Mu) and Akiko Jackson (Mooshu). Gbolahan Adeola. Susanne Schmitt, iconoclast. Felix Reinhuber. Steph Engel. Joy Simpkins, Diane Shapiro, Bonnie Cutler. Michael Shewmaker. Jimin Seo. Kat Savino, who rescued me from spiders. Joanne Knight, for the beach walks. Michael Brown, Jr. Angela Lockhart-Aronoff. Richie Hofmann, who said, "Esther in Paris!" J. P. Grasser. Graham Barnhart. Kara Krewer. Rose Whitmore. Michael Sears. Ryan Black. Yeunhee Cho. Jennifer Franklin. Gauri Awasthi. Kia Corthron. Camille Dungy. With you, I learned precisely what I needed to.

My Undocupoets nation. Anni Liu, Jan-Henry Gray, Aline Mello. Especially Marcelo Hernandez Castillo, Janine Joseph, Christopher "Loma" Soto, Javier Zamora. For making the way.

My radiant students: Maria Castell-Greene, Mila Holt, JoAnne Tillemans, Jennifer Trainor, Jane Rowen, Julia MacNeil, Becky Dougherty, Deborah Barrett, Liane Collins, Arthur Manzi, Eric Glassgold, Martha Browning, you taught me so much.

My first reader, Kevin Fitchett, for reciting "The Fish" on a dock at midnight as he punched a squid.

The geeks who keep me sane: Justin Alvin Moore, my polyphonic Virgil into 5e. Nathan Meeks. Hasan Gürel, Jonathan Martinez-Abbady—periodt. Beatriz Adriana Hicks, Xochilt Vega, Amber Furlong, Jessi Hixson, Abby Gannon, Riley Reyer, Stella Parisi—Romy 4eva. Edie Balogh and Joseph Merino, the glorious bad influences who encouraged me to say yes to the world.

Thank you to Kenny Gordon, your compassion changed my life. Tammy Chen, dear cousin who talked about Mom. Jason Resh—"I can live with it." Nanette Freedland, who taught me the language of family. My second family, Marika Galecki, Lukasz Galecki, and in memory of Daniel.

Ludi Price, the next time I get lost in ten miles of sheep fields, I'll still make my way to you. Hanna Pylväinen, the sobbing room is right this way.

My father, my mother. Vicky and Mark, Thomas and Sasha and Sophia. To my great-grandmother, who could not read, and my great-grandfather, who read to her. To Simone and Siena, I love you.

RECENT TITLES FROM ALICE JAMES BOOKS

If Nothing, Matthew Nienow
Zombie Vomit Mad Libs, Duy Đoàn
The Holy & Broken Bliss, Alicia Ostriker
Wish Ave, Alessandra Lynch
Autobiomythography of, Ayokunle Falomo
Old Stranger: Poems, Joan Larkin
I Don't Want To Be Understood, Joshua Jennifer Espinoza
Canandaigua, Donald Revell
In the Days That Followed, Kevin Goodan
Light Me Down: The New & Collected Poems of Jean Valentine,
Jean Valentine
Song of My Softening, Omotara James
Theophanies, Sarah Ghazal Ali
Orders of Service, Willie Lee Kinard III
The Dead Peasant's Handbook, Brian Turner
The Goodbye World Poem, Brian Turner
The Wild Delight of Wild Things, Brian Turner
I Am the Most Dangerous Thing, Candace Williams
Burning Like Her Own Planet, Vandana Khanna
Standing in the Forest of Being Alive, Katie Farris
Feast, Ina Cariño
Decade of the Brain: Poems, Janine Joseph
American Treasure, Jill McDonough
We Borrowed Gentleness, J. Estanislao Lopez
Brother Sleep, Aldo Amparán
Sugar Work, Katie Marya
Museum of Objects Burned by the Souls in Purgatory, Jeffrey Thomson
Constellation Route, Matthew Olzmann
How to Not Be Afraid of Everything, Jane Wong

Alice James Books is committed to publishing books that matter. The press was founded in 1973 in Boston, Massachusetts to give women access to publishing. As a cooperative, authors performed the day-to-day undertakings of the press. The press continues to expand and grow from its formative roots, guided by its founding values of access, excellence, inclusivity, and collaboration in publishing. Its mission is to publish books that matter and preserve a place of belonging for poets who inspire us. AJB seeks to broaden our collective interpretation of what constitutes the American poetic voice and is dedicated to helping its artists achieve purposeful engagement with broad audiences and communities nationwide. The press was named for Alice James, sister to William and Henry, whose extraordinary gift for writing went unrecognized during her lifetime.

Designed by Zoe Norvell

Printed by Versa Press